CONNECTING WITH WATER IN NATURE

BY ABBY COLICH

T0014836

BLUE OWL
BOOKS

TIPS FOR CAREGIVERS

Social and emotional learning (SEL) helps children manage emotions, learn how to feel empathy, create and achieve goals, and make good decisions. One goal of teaching SEL skills is to help children care for themselves, others, and the world around them. The more time children spend in nature and the more they learn about it, the more likely they will be to appreciate it and receive its emotional benefits.

BEFORE READING

Talk to the reader about activities he or she likes to do in or around water.

Discuss: What kinds of activities do you enjoy that involve water? Do you like to swim or go boating? Do you like to visit a lake or the ocean? What other activities can you think of that involve water?

AFTER READING

Talk to the reader about how he or she feels when doing activities in or around water.

Discuss: How does being near water make you feel? Do you feel excited? Do you feel relaxed and calm?

SEL GOAL

Children may struggle with processing their emotions, and they may lack accessible tools to help them do so. Explain to children that nature can help people feel good. Nature is always available to them, even if they are simply looking out the window or looking at pictures of nature scenes. Encourage children to find a way to feel more connected to water. Whether they are visiting an ocean, listening to a rainstorm, or jumping in a puddle, nature offers many ways to connect with water.

TABLE OF CONTENTS

CHAPTER 1

WATER EVERYWHERE

Water can be found all around Earth! How many places can you think of to find water in nature?

Ponds, lakes, streams, rivers, oceans, and more are made up of water. Water is in the sky as **vapor**. It falls as rain or snow.

Spending time in nature can help you feel calmer. Watching or being in water can be good for your mind and body, too. Water sports are great exercise, which is good for your health.

WATCHING WATER

Scientists have found that simply watching water can be helpful. How? It can inspire feelings of **wonder** and calm. It can help you be more **mindful**. Watching water can give your brain a rest.

CHAPTER 2

BE PREPARED

Safety is the most important thing to keep in mind when around water. Always have an adult's **supervision**. Don't go in water if you don't know how to swim or if you don't know how deep it is. Always wear a life jacket when on a boat or dock.

kayak

Decide where you want to go. Check the weather and dress appropriately. Make sure you have the supplies you need. You may need to rent a boat or other gear. An adult can help you do this.

When spending time in or near water, put away your **devices**. Take in the **scenery** around you. Think about how your body feels. Leave behind thoughts or feelings that are bothering you. Instead, **focus** on the activity you are doing.

TAKE CARE OF WATER

Help keep water and the **wildlife** that live in it clean and safe. When you visit water, never leave your trash behind. Never dump other liquids into a body of water.

CHAPTER 3

WAYS TO ENJOY WATER

There are some ways to enjoy water that don't need a lot of planning. Try having a picnic or going for a walk along a lake or pond. **Gaze** at the still water. Try to keep your body and mind as still as the water.

You can also watch rain fall. Listen to the sound it makes as it hits the ground, roofs, and trees. After the rain, jump in the puddles! How does it feel as you make the water splash?

Swimming is a great way to connect with water. Jump in! Moving through water can feel **exhilarating**. Enjoy the **sensations** as your mind and body relax. Wading or just dipping your toes in are also easy ways to enjoy water.

FINDING A RHYTHM

Repetitive movement can be relaxing. Find a **rhythm** as you swim. How does your breath work with your movement? Do you move differently than you do on land? If your mind wanders, gently bring your thoughts back to these sensations.

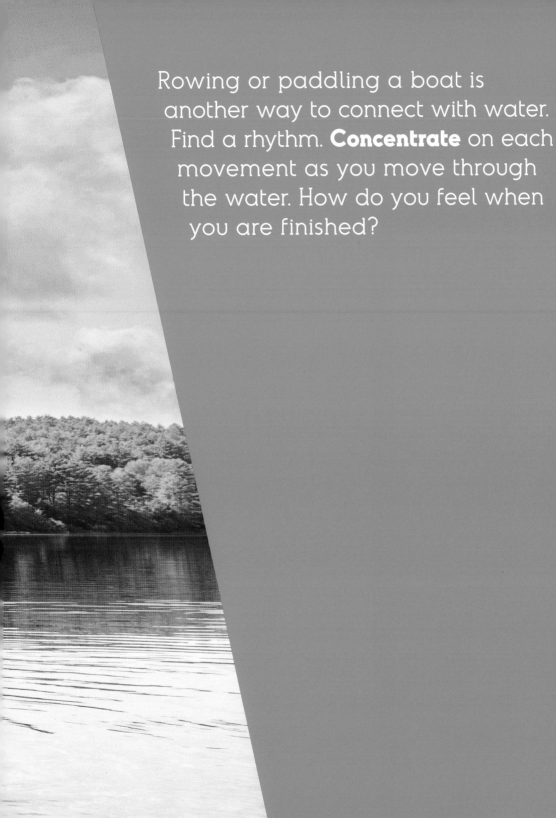

Rowing or paddling a boat is another way to connect with water. Find a rhythm. **Concentrate** on each movement as you move through the water. How do you feel when you are finished?

Fishing can teach you many things. You have to learn how to bait and cast your line. Then you have to be **patient** while you wait for a fish. Be mindful of the water and your surroundings while you wait. When you finally catch a fish, how do you feel?

If you can't visit a place with water, that is OK! Play a recording of the sound of a stream or waves on your device. Then put it down and try to relax. See if it makes you feel calmer. How else can you connect with water?

A SPLASH OF WATER

You can enjoy water even at home. Is it a warm day? Go to your sink. Splash some cold water on your face. Pay attention to how the water feels as it moves across your skin. What do you notice?

GOALS AND TOOLS

GROW WITH GOALS

There are a lot of ways to connect with water.

Goal: The next time you go swimming, try just playing in the water. Let go of your thoughts and have fun splashing around and paying attention to how your body feels as it moves in the water.

Goal: Try walking or hiking near a body of water. Pay attention to what else is around you. What plants and animals do you see? Are there clouds in the sky? What sounds do you hear?

Goal: Find pictures of water scenes that you like. Look at them when you need to focus or quiet your mind.

MINDFULNESS EXERCISE

Play a recording of water sounds, such as rain or ocean waves. Find a quiet place to sit as you listen. Put down any devices. Sit up straight. Close your eyes. Take a few deep breaths. Try to quiet your mind as you focus on the sounds. Do this for a few minutes. Open your eyes. How do you feel after?

GLOSSARY

concentrate
To give all your thought and attention to something.

devices
Pieces of equipment with computers inside, such as smartphones or tablets.

exhilarating
Causing feelings of excitement and happiness.

focus
To concentrate on something.

gaze
To look at something for a long time.

mindful
A mentality achieved by focusing on the present moment and calmly recognizing and accepting your feelings, thoughts, and sensations.

patient
Able to put up with problems or delays without getting angry or upset.

repetitive
Happening again and again.

rhythm
A repeated pattern of sounds or movements.

scenery
Outdoor scenes or views that are pleasing to look at.

sensations
Particular feelings that your body experiences.

supervision
The action of watching someone or something.

vapor
A substance in the form of gas.

wildlife
Living things, especially animals, that live in their natural habitats.

wonder
A feeling caused by something extraordinary.

TO LEARN MORE

FACT SURFER

Finding more information is as easy as 1, 2, 3.

1. Go to www.factsurfer.com

2. Enter "**connectingwithwaterinnature**" into the search box.

3. Choose your book to see a list of websites.

INDEX

Blue Owl Books are published by Jump!, 5357 Penn Avenue South, Minneapolis, MN 55419, www.jumplibrary.com

Copyright © 2021 Jump! International copyright reserved in all countries. No part of this book may be reproduced in any form without written permission from the publisher.

Library of Congress Cataloging-in-Publication Data

Names: Colich, Abby, author.
Title: Connecting with water in nature / by Abby Colich.
Description: Minneapolis: Jump!, Inc., [2021]
Series: Nature heals | Includes index. | Audience: Ages 7–10
Identifiers: LCCN 2020032839 (print)
LCCN 2020032840 (ebook)
ISBN 9781645278313 (hardcover)
ISBN 9781645278320 (paperback)
ISBN 9781645278337 (ebook)
Subjects: LCSH: Nature–Psychological aspects–Juvenile literature. | Water–Juvenile literature. | Nature, Healing power of–Juvenile literature.
Mindfulness (Psychology)–Juvenile literature.
Classification: LCC BF353.5.N37 C646 2021 (print) | LCC BF353.5.N37 (ebook) | DDC 155.4/1891–dc23
LC record available at https://lccn.loc.gov/2020032839
LC ebook record available at https://lccn.loc.gov/2020032840

Editor: Eliza Leahy
Designer: Michelle Sonnek

Photo Credits: My Life Graphic/Shutterstock, cover; Rozochkalvn/Shutterstock, 1; chrisbrignell/iStock, 3; Khoroshunova Olga/Shutterstock, 4; ANURAK PONGPATIMET/Shutterstock, 5; lunamarina/Shutterstock, 6–7; Suzanne Tucker/Shutterstock, 8; Reid Dalland/Shutterstock, 9; AnnGaysorn/Shutterstock, 10–11; xavierarnau/iStock, 12; VMJones/iStock, 13; CasarsaGuru/iStock, 14–15; Romiana Lee/Shutterstock, 16–17; Golden Pixels LLC/Shutterstock, 18–19; Prostock-Studio/iStock, 20–21.

Printed in the United States of America at Corporate Graphics in North Mankato, Minnesota.